One pot
meals

SIMON &
SCHUSTER
ILLUSTRATED

London · New York · Sydney · Toronto

A CBS COMPANY

Sara Buenfeld

First published in Great Britain by
Simon & Schuster UK Ltd, 2011
A CBS Company

Copyright © 2011, Weight Watchers International, Inc.

SIMON AND SCHUSTER
ILLUSTRATED BOOKS
Simon & Schuster UK
222 Gray's Inn Road
London WC1X 8HB
www.simonandschuster.co.uk

Weight Watchers Publications Team: Jane Griffiths,
Cheryl Jackson, Nina McKerlie, Imogen Prescott and
Donna Watts
Simon & Schuster Project Management: WordWorks
Photography: Steve Baxter
Prop styling: Jenny Iggleden
Food preparation: Carol Tennant
Design and typesetting: Richard Proctor

Colour reproduction by Dot Gradations Ltd, UK
Printed and bound in Singapore

A CIP catalogue for this book is available from
the British Library

Pictured on the front cover: Venison Cobbler, page 22

Pictured on the back cover from left to right and
top to bottom: Chicken with Pesto Roast Vegetables,
page 6; Beef and Onion Braise, page 27; Cheesy Spinach
Pudding, page 46; Sponge Pudding with Apricot Sauce,
page 54

ProPoints® value logo: You'll find this easy to read
ProPoints value logo on every recipe throughout this
book. The logo represents the number of **ProPoints** values per
serving each recipe contains. It is not an indication of the
fillingness of a recipe.

Weight Watchers **ProPoints** Weight Loss System is a simple way to
lose weight. As part of the Weight Watchers **ProPoints** plan you'll
enjoy eating delicious, healthy, filling foods that help to keep you
feeling satisfied for longer and in control of your portions.

Filling & Healthy Foods are highlighted in green. Focus on these
foods where you can – they are healthy choices that will help you
to feel satisfied for longer.

V This symbol denotes a vegetarian recipe and assumes that,
where relevant, free range eggs, vegetarian cheese, vegetarian
virtually fat free fromage frais, vegetarian low fat crème fraîche and
vegetarian low fat yogurts are used. Virtually fat free fromage frais,
low fat crème fraîche and low fat yogurts may contain traces of
gelatine so they are not always vegetarian. Please check the labels.

❄ This symbol denotes a dish that can be frozen. Unless otherwise
stated, you can freeze the finished dish for up to 3 months. Defrost
thoroughly and reheat until the dish is piping hot throughout.

Recipe notes

Egg size Medium unless otherwise stated.

Raw eggs Only the freshest eggs should be used. Pregnant
women, the elderly and children should avoid recipes with eggs
which are not fully cooked or raw.

All fruits and vegetables Medium size unless otherwise stated.

Chocolate Use chocolate with a minimum of 70% cocoa solids.

Low fat spread Where a recipe states to use a low fat spread, a
light spread with a fat content of no less than 38% should be used.

Stock Stock cubes should be used in the recipes, unless otherwise
stated. Prepare them according to the packet instructions, unless
directed otherwise.

Microwaves Microwave timings are for an 850 watt microwave
oven.

Recipe timings These are approximate and meant to be
guidelines. Please note that the preparation time includes all the
steps up to and following the main cooking time(s).

Low fat soft cheese Where a recipe states to use a low fat soft
cheese, a soft cheese with a fat content of less than 5% should
be used.

Contents

Introduction

With *One Pot Meals*, the newest cookbook in the Weight Watchers range to accompany the new **ProPoints** plan, you can enjoy a fantastic hassle-free way to cook. Created with you in mind, as well as whoever is washing up, these 60 new recipes are not only delicious, they'll also help you to S-T-R-E-T-C-H your **ProPoints** budget.

The **ProPoints** plan has been designed to work around real life – your life – so you can keep on losing weight whatever situation you find yourself in. It is Weight Watchers most flexible and liveable plan ever – using the latest research in nutritional science.

Whether you're cooking for two, for the family or a whole load more, *One Pot Meals* gives you ideas for tasty dishes that are easy to make and, in many cases, involve only a bit of preparation. Once prepared, you can leave them to cook and get on with all the other things you want to do. Ranging from really simple chicken dishes to delicious desserts, these recipes will give you lots of inspiration for easy meals. With *One Pot Meals* following the **ProPoints** plan is made even easier.

Poultry & game

Chicken and game are ideal for creating easy one pot meals that appeal to everyone. They're so versatile and taste delicious with a wide variety of flavours.

Chicken with pesto roast vegetables

ProPoints values per recipe 69
25 mins prep, 1 hr 35 mins cooking

Serves 6

1.4 kg (3 lb 1 oz) whole chicken
1 large lemon
a few sprigs of fresh herbs, such as sage
　or basil
600 g (1 lb 5 oz) baby new potatoes,
　halved
2 large red onions, cut into wedges
1 head of garlic, separated into cloves
2 red peppers, de-seeded and quartered
400 ml (14 fl oz) hot chicken stock
1 tablespoon white wine vinegar
3 tablespoons green pesto
2 courgettes, sliced
390 g can artichoke hearts in water,
　drained and quartered
calorie controlled cooking spray
salt and freshly ground black pepper

Roast chicken is a real family favourite and this is packed with flavour. Serve with steamed broccoli for no additional *ProPoints* values.

1 Preheat the oven to Gas Mark 4/180°C/fan oven 160°C. Remove all the visible fat from the chicken, especially inside the body cavity, and trim off any loose skin with scissors. Squeeze the juice from the lemon into a bowl and set aside. Put the shells of the lemon inside the body cavity with the sage or basil. Place in a very large roasting tin and season.

2 Scatter the potatoes, onions, garlic and peppers around the chicken. In a jug, stir the stock with the vinegar and 1 tablespoon of the pesto and pour over the chicken and vegetables. Cover with foil and bake for 1 hour. Meanwhile, to make a lemon dressing, mix the lemon juice with the remaining pesto and 2 tablespoons water.

3 Turn the oven up to Gas Mark 7/220°C/fan oven 200°C. Uncover the chicken and scatter around the courgettes and artichoke hearts. Spray with cooking spray and spoon over the pesto and lemon dressing then return to the oven for 35 minutes more until the chicken is cooked and the vegetables are tender.

4 Carve the chicken and serve, without skin, with the vegetables and juices, skimming off any visible fat.

Salsa chicken with beans and rice

ProPoints values per recipe 27

15 mins prep, 18 mins cooking

Serves 2

300 g jar salsa

200 ml (7 fl oz) chicken stock

300 g (10½ oz) butternut squash peeled, de-seeded and cut into chunks

1 red pepper, de-seeded and cut into chunks

75 g (2¾ oz) dried basmati rice

15 g (½ oz) chopped fresh coriander

300 g (10½ oz) skinless boneless chicken breast, cut into chunks

410 g can red kidney beans in water, drained and rinsed

This couldn't be simpler to make. A jar of Mexican salsa forms the base, and depending on your taste you can use a mild or a hot one. Enjoy this dish on its own or with a leafy salad for no additional ProPoints values.

1 Tip half of the jar of salsa into a lidded pan then pour in the stock. Add the squash and pepper, and then cover and simmer for 10 minutes.

2 Add the rice, half the coriander and the chicken then cover the pan and cook gently for about 8 minutes until the rice is tender and the chicken is cooked through.

3 Stir in the beans. Cover and leave for a few minutes to settle. Serve with the remaining salsa and scatter with the rest of the coriander.

Braised turkey with spring vegetables

ProPoints values per recipe 26

15 mins prep, 20 mins cooking

Serves 4

2 tablespoons cornflour

500 ml (18 fl oz) chicken stock

2 tablespoons Dijon mustard

200 g (7 oz) new potatoes, sliced

175 g (6 oz) cauliflower or broccoli florettes, chopped into small pieces

2 teaspoons chopped fresh tarragon

450 g (1 lb) mini skinless turkey breast fillets

100 g (3½ oz) frozen baby broad beans

100 g (3½ oz) frozen petit pois

125 g pack asparagus tips, halved

1 tablespoon half fat crème fraîche

2 tablespoons snipped chives

salt and freshly ground black pepper

In this creamy dish, delicately flavoured with fresh tarragon, vegetables and potatoes are cooked together with turkey fillets.

1 Blend the cornflour with 3 tablespoons of water. Pour the stock into a large, deep, lidded, non stick saucepan. Add the mustard and then the cornflour mixture. Stir over the heat until thickened.

2 Add the potatoes and cauliflower or broccoli to the pan with half of the tarragon and then season. Cover and cook gently for 10 minutes, stirring occasionally.

3 Add the turkey to the pan, scatter over the beans, petit pois and asparagus tips, then cover and cook gently for about 8–10 minutes so that the turkey is just cooked and the vegetables are tender.

4 Add the crème fraîche, chives and remaining tarragon. Season then ladle into bowls.

Spice box chicken with banana sambal

ProPoints values per recipe 17

20 mins prep, 50 mins cooking

                                    Serves 4

3 large onions**, quartered**

4 garlic cloves

2.5 cm (1 inch) fresh root ginger**,**
  chopped roughly

½ teaspoon cumin seeds

½ teaspoon ground turmeric

4 cardamom pods

2 teaspoons ground coriander

2 large fresh red chillies**, de-seeded**
  and chopped finely

2 tablespoons plain flour

1 tablespoon tomato purée

425 ml (15 fl oz) chicken stock

500 g (1 lb 2 oz) skinless boneless chicken
  breasts**, cubed**

20 g packet fresh coriander**, chopped**

For the banana sambal

1 small red onion**, chopped finely**

½ cucumber**, de-seeded and diced**

2 bananas**, diced**

grated zest and juice of 1 lime

Serve this authentic curry with 50 g (1¾ oz) dried brown rice per person, cooked according to the packet instructions, for an extra 5 **ProPoints** values per serving. Or try serving with one Weight Watchers mini plain naan bread per person for an additional 3 **ProPoints** values per serving.

1 Put the onions in a food processor with the garlic and ginger. Whizz until as smooth as possible and then pour in 150 ml (5 fl oz) water and whizz again.

2 Heat a large, lidded, non stick pan. Tip in the spices and toast for a minute to release the flavours. Pour in the onion mixture and all but 1 teaspoon of the chopped chilli. Add the flour and tomato purée and stir well. Gradually blend in the chicken stock then cover and leave to simmer for 40 minutes, stirring occasionally, until the mixture is pulpy and the onions are completely cooked.

3 Add the chicken and half of the fresh coriander. Cover and cook very gently for 8 minutes.

4 Meanwhile, mix together all the sambal ingredients with the remaining chilli and fresh coriander and serve beside the chicken.

Cook's tip Using puréed onion, garlic and ginger to add texture as well as flavour is a classic Indian technique. Do make sure the onions are fully cooked though – if not, the mixture will taste a little bitter.

Sloppy Joe

6 ProPoints value

ProPoints values per recipe 35
20 mins prep, 50 mins cooking
❄ without the bread   **Serves 6**

calorie controlled cooking spray
1 large onion, chopped
4 garlic cloves; 3 chopped and 1 whole
    but peeled
2 tablespoons mild or hot chilli powder
1 teaspoon smoked paprika
1 teaspoon ground cumin
2 teaspoons chopped fresh thyme,
    plus extra for sprinkling if desired
500 g (1 lb 2 oz) turkey mince
2 tablespoons plain flour
425 ml (15 fl oz) chicken stock
400 g can cherry tomatoes
4 celery sticks, chopped
4 carrots, peeled and chopped
1 large red pepper, de-seeded and
    chopped
250 g pack closed cup mushrooms,
    chopped
100 g (3½ oz) frozen sweetcorn
125 g (4½ oz) French stick, cut into
    12 thick slices
salt and freshly ground black pepper

This is really quite hot, so choose the mild chilli powder if you'd prefer this dish to be less fiery.

1 Heat a large, lidded, flameproof and ovenproof dish and spray with the cooking spray. Add the onion and chopped garlic, cover and cook over a low to medium heat, stirring occasionally for about 5 minutes. If they start to stick, add a splash of water.

2 Stir the spices and thyme into the onion. Add the turkey mince, breaking up the mince with a wooden spoon, and flour. Pour in the chicken stock, then heat, stirring, until bubbling and thickened.

3 Tip in the tomatoes, celery, carrots, pepper, mushrooms and sweetcorn. Season and then cover the pan and leave to simmer, stirring occasionally, for 30 minutes until the vegetables are tender. Preheat the oven to Gas Mark 6/200°C/fan oven 180°C.

4 Rub the whole garlic clove over the bread slices and then spray with the cooking spray. Arrange the bread garlic side up on top of the mince and bake in the oven for 15–20 minutes until golden. Scatter with the thyme, if using, and serve.

Try this Instead of topping the mince with slices of garlic bread, you can replace them with a 225 g (8 oz) potato per person, baked in its skin, for 5 *ProPoints* values per serving.

Plum duck with watercress

ProPoints values per recipe 8

Takes 20 mins

Serves 2

2 tablespoons Chinese plum sauce

1 tablespoon soy sauce

1 cm (½ inch) fresh root ginger,
  chopped finely

1 garlic clove, sliced

calorie controlled cooking spray

150 g (5½ oz) skinless duck breast fillet,
  sliced thinly

2 carrots, peeled, halved and sliced
  thinly on the diagonal

1 celery stick, sliced thinly

1 red onion, cubed

a handful of watercress

freshly ground black pepper

The secret to a good stir fry is to have all the ingredients prepared before you start cooking. Serve with 60 g (2 oz) dried rice per person, cooked according to the packet instructions, for an additional 6 **ProPoints** values per serving.

1 In a bowl, mix the plum sauce and soy sauce with 3 tablespoons of water. Add the ginger and garlic then set aside. Heat a lidded wok or non stick frying pan and spray with the cooking spray. Add the duck season with black pepper and cook very briefly, until the duck just turns brown. Remove from the pan and set aside.

2 Add the carrots, celery and onion to the pan, add a little water then cover and steam fry for 5 minutes so the vegetables soften, but still have a little bite.

3 Pour in the plum sauce mixture and allow it to bubble then toss in the duck and watercress. Serve immediately.

Cook's tip When using salty ingredients such as soy sauce, there is no need to add additional salt when seasoning.

Chinese chicken and sweetcorn soup

ProPoints values per recipe 17

Takes 10 mins

Serves 2

100 g (3½ oz) skinless boneless
  chicken breast

340 g can sweetcorn, drained
  or 285 g (10 oz) frozen sweetcorn

600 ml (20 fl oz) chicken stock

1 tablespoon cornflour

2 spring onions, shredded

1 egg, beaten

This Chinese restaurant favourite can be made at home in a matter of minutes. The thick texture makes it very satisfying as a lunch or a light supper, especially if you're in a hurry.

1 Place the chicken breast between two sheets of cling film then hit firmly with the base of a saucepan or a rolling pin to flatten. Cut the chicken into thin strips.

2 Put the sweetcorn in a pan then pour in the stock. Mix the cornflour with 2 tablespoons of water and add it to the pan. Heat, stirring, until bubbling and thickened.

3 Add the chicken and spring onions, cook for about 1 minute (the chicken cooks quickly as soon as it is added), then drizzle in the egg and stir to create the classic Chinese egg threads in the soup. The egg will cook instantly as it hits the hot soup. Serve in warmed bowls.

Try this This is ideal for using up the last of a cooked chicken. For some extra flavour, add ½ a teaspoon of sesame oil, for an additional 1 **ProPoints** value per serving.

4 ProPoints value

Layered potato bake

ProPoints values per recipe 39
20 mins prep, 1 hr cooking

Serves 4

850 ml (1½ pints) skimmed milk
40 g (1½ oz) plain flour
15 g (½ oz) low fat spread
1 tablespoon English mustard
a pinch of freshly grated nutmeg
800 g (1 lb 11 oz) potatoes, scrubbed
well and sliced thinly
400 g (14 oz) leeks, washed and
sliced thinly
3 garlic cloves, sliced
200 g pack smoked turkey rashers,
sliced thinly
100 g (3½ oz) baby spinach leaves
40 g (1½ oz) half fat Cheddar cheese,
grated
salt and freshly ground black pepper

This is similar to a gratin dauphinois in which potatoes are sliced and layered. Serve with a crisp green salad, for no additional *ProPoints* values.

1 Preheat the oven to Gas Mark 5/190°C/fan oven 170°C. Pour the milk into a lidded flameproof and ovenproof casserole dish. Add the flour, low fat spread, mustard and nutmeg and season to taste. Stir continuously over the heat until thickened then remove from the heat.

2 Layer in the potatoes, leeks, garlic, turkey rashers and spinach, ending with a layer of potatoes and press down in the dish.

3 Scatter over the cheese. Bake with the lid on for 30 minutes. Remove the lid and bake for 30 minutes longer to brown the top. Serve immediately.

Cook's tip Leeks can contain quite a lot of grit. The best way to remove it is to slit the top of the leek so you can separate the leaves then wash them under cold running water to flush out the grit before slicing them.

Chicken pot noodle

ProPoints values per recipe 20
Takes 15 mins

Serves 2

700 ml (1¼ pints) chicken stock
1½ teaspoons Madras curry paste
120 g (4½ oz) dried medium egg
noodles
750 g (1 lb 10 oz) frozen ready mixed
vegetables such as green beans,
broccoli, cauliflower and carrots
100 g (3½ oz) skinless boneless chicken
breast, sliced then cut into thin strips
4 tablespoons chopped fresh coriander
4 spring onions, shredded

If you want something fast and filling, try this store cupboard recipe that uses mixed vegetables from the freezer.

1 Pour the stock into a lidded pan and add the curry paste. Bring to the boil then add the noodles and frozen vegetables. Cover and cook for 5 minutes.

2 Add the chicken, coriander and spring onions and cook for a minute or two more (the chicken will cook quickly on impact with the heat). Serve in bowls.

Try this If you have any leftover chicken or meat from a roast, this recipe is a great way for using it up as a little can go a long way. Remove all traces of skin first.

Pheasant and mushroom casserole

ProPoints values per recipe 22

20 mins prep, 35 mins cooking

Serves 4

calorie controlled cooking spray

25 g (1 oz) lean smoked back bacon,
    chopped

4 x 80 g (3 oz) skinless boneless
    pheasant breasts

12 small shallots, peeled

3 carrots, peeled and diced finely

2 celery sticks, diced finely

3 garlic cloves, sliced thinly

3 tablespoons red wine

1 tablespoon red wine vinegar

500 ml (18 fl oz) chicken stock

2 tablespoons tomato purée

1 teaspoon chopped fresh thyme

150 g pack baby button mushrooms

3 tablespoons chopped fresh parsley

salt and freshly ground black pepper

Many supermarkets now sell game when it's in season and it makes an impressive meal when you're entertaining friends. Serve with 150 g (5½ oz) new **potatoes** per person, for an additional 3 **ProPoints** values per serving.

1 Heat a lidded flameproof casserole dish. Spray with the cooking spray and fry the bacon and pheasant until they just start to colour. Add the shallots, carrots, celery and garlic. Stir well then pour in the wine and vinegar.

2 Add the stock to the pan then stir in the tomato purée, thyme and mushrooms. Season then cover and leave to simmer for 35 minutes until the pheasant is tender. Stir in the parsley and serve immediately.

Try this When pheasant breasts are out of season, use 450 g (1 lb) skinless boneless chicken thighs. Cut them each into about three pieces and add 10 more minutes to the cooking time in step two. The **ProPoints** values per serving will be 7.

Lemon chicken Marrakesh

ProPoints values per recipe 54
10 mins prep, 50 mins cooking
✿ without the couscous   **Serves 4**

1 lemon

2 red onions, chopped

1 large fennel bulb, chopped

1 large red pepper, de-seeded and cubed

600 g (1 lb 5 oz) skinless boneless chicken thighs, trimmed of all visible fat

20 (50 g/1¾ oz) pimento stuffed olives (in brine), drained

2 large red chillies, sliced

2 garlic cloves, sliced

1 teaspoon ground paprika

2 teaspoons ground cumin

1 tablespoon ground coriander

1 litre (1¾ pints) chicken stock

200 g (7 oz) dried couscous

4 tablespoons chopped fresh parsley or coriander (optional)

salt and freshly ground black pepper

The couscous in this satisfying dish is added at the last minute to soak up the delicious juices, but it can also be served separately.

1 Cut the peel from the lemon with a vegetable peeler and then slice it into matchstick shreds. Put it in a lidded flameproof casserole dish with the onions, fennel, pepper, chicken, olives, chillies, garlic, spices and seasoning. Squeeze the juice from the lemon and reserve.

2 Pour the stock into the pan then cover and simmer for 45 minutes until the chicken is really tender.

3 Tip in the couscous, lemon juice and parsley or coriander, if using. Turn off the heat and leave for 5 minutes to plump up the couscous before serving.

Try this If you enjoy trying new ingredients, you may like to try Moroccan preserved lemons which are sold in most supermarkets. Rinse off the salt, chop finely and use to replace the fresh lemon zest and juice in this recipe. The **ProPoints** values will be the same.

Freezer tip You can freeze this before adding the couscous. Thaw thoroughly then reheat in a pan and add the couscous as above in step 3.

Marinated chicken with sweet potatoes

ProPoints values per recipe 22

20 mins prep + 1 hr marinating,
35 mins cooking   **Serves 2**

2 small red onions**, cut into wedges**
grated zest and juice of ½ a lemon
2 tablespoons low fat plain yogurt
½ teaspoon smoked paprika
1 teaspoon fresh thyme leaves
450 g (1 lb) skinless chicken drumsticks
calorie controlled cooking spray
300 g (10½ oz) sweet potatoes**, unpeeled
    and cut into wedges**
1 large red pepper**, de-seeded and cut
    into large chunks**
6 whole garlic cloves
a generous handful of rocket leaves
salt and freshly ground black pepper
lemon wedges, to serve

The spicy yogurt marinade in this recipe not only flavours the
delicate meat, it also prevents it from drying out.

1 Put a couple of the onion wedges in a food processor, with the
lemon zest and juice, yogurt, paprika, thyme and seasoning and
whizz until smooth. Pour over the chicken and leave to marinate
for 1 hour at room temperature, or in the fridge for longer.
2 Preheat the oven to Gas Mark 6/200°C/fan oven 180°C. Spray
a large non stick baking tray with the cooking spray and scatter
over the sweet potatoes, red pepper, remaining onion wedges and
garlic. Add the marinated drumsticks and spray lightly with the
cooking spray again to encourage the vegetables to brown.
3 Roast for 30–35 minutes until the chicken and vegetables are
cooked through. Serve topped with the rocket leaves and lemon
wedges for squeezing over.

Cook's tip To remove the skin from a chicken drumstick,
hold the skin at the thick end and pull it down so the skin is
virtually inside out, but still attached at the thin boney end.
Then snip the skin off with scissors to completely remove it.

Marvellous meat

Impress your friends and please the family too with these easy recipes. You can rustle up a stir fry, toss together an exotic salad or slow cook a satisfying stew.

Saucy Spanish meatballs

ProPoints values per recipe 17

20 mins prep, 15 mins cooking

 Serves 4

400 g pack Weight Watchers premium pork sausages

50 g (1¾ oz) carrot, peeled and grated finely

½ teaspoon dried oregano

calorie controlled cooking spray

300 ml (10 fl oz) passata

500 ml (18 fl oz) chicken stock

2 tablespoons chopped fresh thyme

150 g (5½ oz) open cup mushrooms, sliced

1 teaspoon smoked paprika

1 red pepper, cut into strips

20 pitted green olives

175 g (6 oz) baby spinach leaves

freshly ground black pepper

Meatballs are always popular, especially with the younger members of the family. Serve with 40 g (1½ oz) dried pasta per person, cooked according to the packet instructions and stirred through just before serving, for 4 **ProPoints** values per serving.

1 Remove the skins from the sausages and discard, then put the sausage meat in a large bowl and work in the carrot and oregano with plenty of black pepper. Using wet hands, shape into 24 meatballs, each about the size of a walnut.

2 Heat a large, lidded, non stick pan and spray with the cooking spray. Add the meatballs and fry gently to colour them, shaking the pan every now and then to make sure they don't stick.

3 Pour the passata into the pan with the stock, thyme, mushrooms, paprika, pepper and olives. Stir gently then cover and leave to simmer for 15 minutes.

4 Add the spinach, stir gently until wilted, then serve.

Try this You could also serve this with 60 g (2 oz) dried brown rice per person, cooked according to the packet instructions, for 6 **ProPoints** values per serving.

Asian beef and mango salad

ProPoints values per recipe 8

Takes 20 mins

Serves 2

calorie controlled cooking spray

200 g (7 oz) lean fillet steak**, trimmed of all visible fat, and sliced**

2 spring onions**, sliced diagonally**

¼ cucumber**, halved, de-seeded and sliced**

1 Little Gem lettuce**, separated into leaves**

2 tablespoons chopped fresh mint

1 small mango**, peeled, stoned and cut into chunks**

freshly ground black pepper

For the dressing

grated zest and juice of 1 lime

1 tablespoon fish sauce

1 teaspoon soy sauce

1 tablespoon sweet chilli sauce

½ red chilli**, chopped finely**

1 garlic clove**, chopped finely**

This warm salad, which is mixed with a very tasty Thai style dressing, is packed full of flavour. Serve with 60 g (2 oz) dried brown rice per person, for an extra 6 **ProPoints** values per serving.

1 Make the dressing by mixing together the zest and juice of the lime, the fish sauce, soy sauce, chilli sauce, chilli and garlic. Set aside.

2 Heat a large wok, spray with the cooking spray and stir fry the beef for just a few seconds so it is cooked, but still rare. Remove the pan from the heat and add the spring onions and dressing to the pan. Season with black pepper, then toss well to coat the beef.

3 Add the remaining ingredients and toss again. Serve quickly to prevent the lettuce from wilting.

Malaysian pork with pineapple

ProPoints values per recipe 30
20 mins prep, 30 mins cooking
❄
Serves 6

1 large onion, quartered

700 ml (1¼ pints) chicken stock

1 tablespoon ground coriander

1 teaspoon turmeric

½ teaspoon ground white pepper

2 star anise

1 cinnamon stick

1 cm (½ inch) fresh root ginger, chopped

2 garlic cloves, sliced and then sliced
again into matchsticks

1 cucumber, peeled, de-seeded and
sliced thickly at an angle

1 tablespoon salt

4 strips lime zest

227 g can pineapple chunks in
natural juice

400 ml can reduced fat coconut milk

2 large red peppers, de-seeded and
cut into strips

1–2 red chillies, de-seeded and sliced

1 tablespoon Thai fish sauce

30 g pack fresh coriander, leaves and
stalks separated and both chopped

500 g (1 lb 2 oz) lean pork fillet,
sliced into rounds

A fragrant oriental dish like this is ideal for entertaining friends. The recipe contains quite a lot of salt, but don't be alarmed – it's only used to draw the moisture out of the cucumber and then thoroughly rinsed off.

1 Put the onion in the food processor with the chicken stock and whizz until really smooth. Tip into a large lidded pan and bring to the boil. Reduce the heat, add the ground and whole spices, ginger and garlic, then cover the pan and leave to simmer for 20 minutes.

2 Meanwhile, toss the cucumber with the salt and set aside to allow the salt to draw out the excess water.

3 When the onion mixture has simmered for 20 minutes, stir in the lime zest, the juice from the pineapple and the coconut milk, then stir in the peppers, chillies, fish sauce, chopped coriander stalks and pork. Cover the pan and cook gently for 10 minutes.

4 Rinse the cucumber to remove all traces of salt, then stir it into the pan with the remaining coriander, and the pineapple. Cook for just a minute to warm the pineapple, then serve.

Venison cobbler

ProPoints values per recipe 52

30 mins prep, 1¾ hours cooking

❄ without the cobbler   **Serves 6**

calorie controlled cooking spray

600 g (1 lb 5 oz) diced venison

4 garlic cloves**, chopped**

2 tablespoons plain flour

300 ml (10 fl oz) low alchohol beer

600 ml (20 fl oz) beef stock

2 tablespoons grainy mustard

300 g (10½ oz) Chantenay carrots**,**
   ends trimmed

450 g (1 lb) celeriac**, peeled and cubed**

300 g pack shallots**, peeled**

250 g (9 oz) flat mushrooms**, halved**
   and sliced thickly

2 bay leaves

salt and freshly ground black pepper

For the cobbler

200 g (7 oz) self raising flour, plus
   1 tablespoon for dusting

1 teaspoon baking powder

a good pinch of mixed herbs

15 g (½ oz) low fat spread

150 ml (5 fl oz) skimmed milk

Venison is a very lean meat, with a much richer taste than beef. Wild venison is only available in the autumn and winter but farmed venison is available all year. Serve with a zero **ProPoints** value green vegetable, such as broccoli.

1 Preheat the oven to Gas Mark 3/160°C/fan oven 140°C. Heat a large, lidded, non stick flameproof and ovenproof casserole dish and spray with the cooking spray. Fry the meat in batches to brown. Remove from the pan then add the garlic and flour. Stir briefly then pour in the beer, stock, and mustard, stirring all the time until thickened.

2 Add the meat back into the pan, followed by all the vegetables and the bay leaves, then season with black pepper. Cover and cook in the oven for 1½ hours. Check that the meat is tender and if not, cook for a little while longer – generally, venison cooks more quickly than beef.

3 To make the cobbler, mix together the flour, baking powder, herbs and seasoning then rub in the low fat spread. Add the milk and mix to a soft dough with the blade of a round end knife. Lightly dust a clean work surface with 1 tablespoon of the flour. Tip the cobbler mixture out on to the work surface, then roll and stamp out six rounds, about 7 cm (2¾ inches) each.

4 Remove the casserole dish from the oven, turn the heat up to Gas Mark 7/220°C/fan oven 200°C, and arrange the rounds on top of the stew. Return to the oven and bake for 15 minutes or until the scones are risen and cooked.

Cook's tips The Chantenay carrots look attractive, but if you prefer, you can use ordinary ones, cut into chunky sticks.
   And if you don't like the slightly bitter edge that beer brings, you can replace it with stock and use a total of 900 ml (1½ pints) for the same **ProPoints** values per serving.

Try this You might like to use 600 g (1 lb 5 oz) cubed lean braising steak, instead of the venison, for 8 **ProPoints** values per serving.

9
ProPoints
value

Dorset pork pot roast

ProPoints values per recipe 34
20 mins prep, 2 hrs 10 mins cooking
Serves 4

1 tablespoon cider vinegar
4 garlic cloves, 1 crushed and 3 sliced finely
2 teaspoons grainy mustard
2 teaspoons clear honey
4 x 110 g (4 oz) lean pork loin steaks, trimmed of all visible fat
500 g (1 lb 2 oz) potatoes, scrubbed well and sliced thinly
1 leek, sliced thinly
1 large Bramley apple, peeled and chopped
2 teaspoons chopped fresh sage
250 g (9 oz) Savoy cabbage, shredded
500 ml (18 fl oz) chicken stock
calorie controlled cooking spray
salt and freshly ground black pepper

The potatoes are cooked with sage and apple for a tangy taste that goes so well with the marinated pork loin steaks. Serve as it is or with an extra zero **ProPoints** value vegetable on the side.

1 Preheat the oven to Gas Mark 3/160°C/fan oven 140°C. In a small, shallow bowl, mix together the cider vinegar, crushed garlic, mustard and honey. Add the pork and toss well. Set aside to marinate until ready to cook.

2 Meanwhile, mix together the potatoes, leek, apple, sliced garlic, sage and seasoning, then pile half into a large, deep, lidded casserole dish. Scatter over the cabbage then top with the rest of the potato mixture. Pour over the stock then spray with a little cooking spray. Cover and cook in the oven for 2 hours until the vegetables are tender.

3 Turn the oven up to Gas Mark 6/200°C/fan oven 180°C. Remove the lid from the casserole dish and arrange the pork steaks on top. Spoon over any marinade left in the bowl then return the lid to the dish. Bake it for 10 minutes, taking care not to overcook the pork or it will be dry and tough. Serve immediately.

Penne with mushrooms and ham

ProPoints values per recipe 24
Takes 25 mins
Serves 4

200 g (7 oz) dried penne
2 leeks, halved and shredded
calorie controlled cooking spray
2 garlic cloves, chopped finely
125 g (4½ oz) large closed cup mushrooms, halved and sliced
2 teaspoons English mustard
100 g (3½ oz) wafer thin smoked ham, shredded
15 g (½ oz) Parmesan cheese, grated coarsely
3 tablespoons torn fresh basil leaves
salt and freshly ground black pepper

Cooking the leeks with the pasta makes them soft and melty and creates a lovely onion sauce for this quick family supper.

1 Bring a large lidded pan of water to the boil, add the pasta and leeks then cook according to the packet instructions until the pasta is al dente, about 12 minutes. Drain, but reserve a mugful of the cooking liquid.

2 Spray the pan with the cooking spray, add the garlic and mushrooms and toss around the pan until the mushrooms start to soften and cook. If the mixture seems a little dry, add a splash of the reserved cooking liquid.

3 Tip the leeks and pasta back into the pan and add the mustard, ham and seasoning. Toss well and moisten with some pasta water if it needs it then add the Parmesan and basil. Serve straight away.

Marvellous meat

Spicy lamb and chick pea soup

ProPoints values per recipe 25

20 mins prep, 15 mins cooking

❄ **Serves 6**

calorie controlled cooking spray

175 g (6 oz) lean lamb leg steak, visible
fat removed, and diced finely

1 large onion, halved and sliced

2 garlic cloves, chopped

½ teaspoon crushed chilli flakes

1 tablespoon ground coriander

1½ teaspoons ground cumin

1 teaspoon ground turmeric

50 g (1¾ oz) dried brown rice

2.25 litres (4 pints) beef stock

2 bay leaves

3 celery sticks, sliced thinly

30 g pack fresh coriander, chopped

400 g can chick peas in water, drained

grated zest and juice of ½ a lemon

3 tablespoons chopped fresh mint

salt and freshly ground black pepper

This is a great soup to freeze in portions, ready to bring out for a filling lunch.

1 Heat a large lidded non stick pan, spray with the cooking spray, and add the lamb, onion and garlic. Fry for 5 minutes, stirring every now and then.

2 Add the chilli flakes, ground spices and rice. Stir for a few seconds then pour in the stock with the bay leaves, celery and half the coriander. Season and then cover and leave to simmer for 15 minutes until the rice is just tender.

3 Add the chick peas, remaining coriander, lemon zest and juice and mint, and return to the boil. Serve in warmed bowls.

Turkish stuffed peppers

Bulgur wheat and lean minced beef mixed with mint and currants make an excellent filling for roast peppers. Serve with a tomato, cucumber and onion salad for no extra **ProPoints** values.

50 g (1¾ oz) dried bulgur wheat

25 g (1 oz) currants

3 tablespoons tomato purée

1 garlic clove, **crushed finely**

½ teaspoon dried mint

300 ml (10 fl oz) hot chicken stock

300 g (10½ oz) extra lean minced beef

2 spring onions, **chopped finely**

**a good pinch of ground cinnamon
    or allspice**

40 g (1½ oz) feta light, crumbled

4 large red or orange peppers

6 cherry tomatoes, **halved**

calorie controlled cooking spray

salt and freshly ground black pepper

1 Preheat the oven to Gas Mark 6/200°C/fan oven 180°C. Put the bulgur wheat, currants, tomato purée, garlic and mint in a bowl and pour over the stock. Stir well then leave to soak for 10 minutes.

2 Stir in the beef, breaking it up with a wooden spoon, and then add the spring onions, cinnamon and feta. Season lightly.

3 Halve the peppers through the stalk and carefully remove the seeds. Place on a baking tray then pile in the stuffing and push in the cherry tomatoes on top.

4 Spray with the cooking spray and then bake in the oven for 50 minutes to 1 hour until the peppers are nice and tender.

Lamb with cinnamon and apricots

This is based on a Moroccan recipe which uses dried apricots, but apricots canned in natural juice have zero **ProPoints** values so are well worth using instead. Serve with 60 g (2 oz) dried basmati rice per person or 60 g (2 oz) dried couscous per person, cooked according to the packet instructions, for an additional 6 **ProPoints** values per serving.

411 g can apricot halves in natural juice

calorie controlled cooking spray

3 small red onions, **sliced into rings**

**4 x 500 g (1 lb 2 oz) lean lamb leg steaks,
    trimmed of all visible fat, and cubed**

1 tablespoon ground coriander

2 teaspoons ground cumin

425 ml (15 fl oz) vegetable or beef stock

3 garlic cloves, **crushed**

2 tablespoons grated fresh root ginger

2 tablespoons tomato purée

1 cinnamon stick

1 large aubergine, **cubed**

1 tablespoon chopped fresh parsley

salt and freshly ground black pepper

1 Drain the apricot halves, reserving the juice. Set aside 12 halves and finely chop the rest. Heat a large lidded pan and spray with the cooking spray. Add the onions, lamb and ground spices. Stir for a few seconds then pour in the stock, the chopped apricots and the reserved juice.

2 Add the garlic, ginger, tomato purée and cinnamon stick then stir in the aubergine. Season then cover the pan and simmer for 45 minutes until tender.

3 Stir in the reserved apricot halves and the parsley. Heat through and then serve.

Beef and onion braise

ProPoints values per recipe 27
20 mins prep, 2½ hrs cooking

❄   **Serves 4**

calorie controlled cooking spray

3 small onions, cut into wedges

4 x 150 g (5½ oz) lean braising steaks,
**   trimmed of all visible fat**

2 tablespoons plain flour

700 ml (1¼ pints) beef stock

300 g (10½ oz) carrots, peeled and cut
**   into thick sticks**

3 garlic cloves, sliced

2 tablespoons tomato purée

1 tablespoon Worcestershire sauce

1 bouqet garni or ½ a teaspoon of mixed
**   dried herbs and two bay leaves**

350 g (12 oz) large closed cup
**   mushrooms, sliced thickly**

freshly ground black pepper

While the beef is cooking, you might like to also bake a 225 g (8 oz) potato per person in its skin to serve with this rich-tasting braise, for an extra 5 **ProPoints** values per serving.

1 Preheat the oven to Gas Mark 3/160°C/fan oven 140°C. On the hob, heat a large, lidded, non stick, flameproof and ovenproof casserole dish over a medium-high heat. Spray with the cooking spray, add the onions and cook for 4 minutes on each side until coloured but not burnt. Remove and set aside.

2 Season the steaks with black pepper, add to the dish and brown on each side, only to colour them, not to cook them. Remove and set aside.

3 Stir the plain flour into the dish then gradually add the stock, stirring all the time to prevent lumps from forming. When thickened, add all the remaining ingredients. Return the onions and steaks to the dish. Cover and cook in the oven for 2½ hours until the meat is tender. Remove the bouquet garni or bay leaves before serving.

Easy beef stir fry

ProPoints values per recipe 8
Takes 20 mins

Serves 1

1½ tablespoons **teriyaki marinade**
1 garlic clove, **chopped**
½ cm (¼ inch) fresh root ginger,
    chopped finely
1 teaspoon **cornflour**
a good pinch of Chinese five spice powder
2 teaspoons **honey**
calorie controlled cooking spray
100 g (3½ oz) lean fillet steak, **sliced
    into strips**
1 small red onion, **cut into wedges**
½ small red pepper, **de-seeded and cut
    into strips**
4 baby corn, **cut lengthways then in half**
3 small broccoli **florettes**
1 Chinese leaf, **shredded**
freshly ground black pepper

Don't worry if you don't have all the vegetables in the list. You can vary them depending on what you have in the fridge, providing they are vegetables with zero **ProPoints** values. Serve with 40 g (1½ oz) dried noodles, cooked according to packet instructions, for an extra 4 **ProPoints** values.

1 In a bowl, mix together the teriyaki marinade with the garlic, ginger, cornflour, Chinese five spice, honey and 100 ml (3½ fl oz) of water. Set aside.

2 Heat a lidded non stick wok and spray with the cooking spray. Add the beef strips and stir fry for about 30 seconds to a minute until the beef is just starting to turn from pink to brown – you still want the meat to be a little rare. Remove and set aside.

3 Stir the cornflour mixture to mix it again, pour it into the wok and stir over the heat with a wooden spoon until bubbling and thickened. Stir in the onion, pepper, baby corn and broccoli. Season with the black pepper then cover the pan for a few minutes to help cook the vegetables – you still want them to be a little crunchy. Return the beef to the wok and toss through the shredded Chinese leaf then serve.

Cook's tips Any leftover Chinese leaves can be added to noodle dishes, steamed and coated with soy or oyster sauce as a side dish or shredded into salads. They are useful because they'll keep in the fridge for up to 5 days.

You can replace the fillet steak with the same amount of rump steak for 9 **ProPoints** values per serving.

Quick lamb tabbouleh

ProPoints values per recipe 17
Takes 25 mins

Serves 2

90 g (3¼ oz) 0% fat Greek yogurt

2 garlic cloves, crushed

½ teaspoon ground coriander

¼ teaspoon ground cumin

175 g (6 oz) lean lamb leg steaks, visible
    fat removed, cut into large chunks

425 ml (15 fl oz) hot chicken stock

75 g (2¾ oz) dried bulgur wheat

grated zest and juice of 1 lemon

2 tablespoons chopped fresh mint,
    plus 1 teaspoon

calorie controlled cooking spray

1 small red onion, chopped finely

2 large tomatoes, chopped

¼ cucumber, diced finely

salt and freshly ground black pepper

Serve this Middle Eastern style salad on its own or with one medium pitta bread (60 g/2 oz) per person, warmed and cut into strips, for 4 **ProPoints** values per serving.

1 In a shallow bowl, mix 2 tablespoons of the yogurt with half the garlic, the spices and a little seasoning. Add the lamb and stir until well coated, then set aside.

2 Put the stock and bulgur wheat in a non stick wok and boil for 8 minutes until the stock has been absorbed. Tip into a bowl and set aside. Rinse the wok.

3 To make the dressing, mix 1 tablespoon of lemon juice into the remaining yogurt with 1 tablespoon water, the rest of the garlic, the teaspoon of mint and a little seasoning.

4 Heat the wok and then spray with the cooking spray. Add the lamb and stir fry for just a few minutes so it is cooked, but still a little pink and juicy in the centre. Add the bulgur wheat with the lemon zest and the juice of half a lemon, the onion, tomatoes, cucumber and the 2 tablespoons of mint. Toss well and serve while still warm with the dressing.

Fish & seafood

Discover how fabulous fish and seafood taste when stirred through a risotto, added to a stir fry or baked in a delicious savoury crumble.

Fresh salmon Provençal

ProPoints values per recipe 23

Takes 45 mins

Serves 4

1 large onion**, chopped finely**

500 ml (18 fl oz) fish stock

2 garlic cloves**, sliced**

2 tablespoons tomato ketchup

500 g (1 lb 2 oz) tomatoes**, chopped**

1 large orange pepper**, quartered
    and sliced**

2 courgettes**, sliced**

1 teaspoon balsamic vinegar

**4 teaspoons small capers in brine,
    drained**

2 tablespoons chopped fresh basil**,
    plus a few leaves to garnish**

4 x 115 g (4¼ oz) skinless salmon fillets

salt and freshly ground black pepper

Serve this tasty dish with 150 g (5½ oz) new potatoes per person for an additional 3 *ProPoints* values per serving, or a 30 g (1¼ oz) slice of crusty bread per person, for an extra 2 *ProPoints* values per serving.

1 Put the onion in a large lidded casserole dish, preferably a shallow one, with the stock, garlic and ketchup and bring to the boil. Reduce the heat, cover and leave to simmer for 10 minutes.

2 Add the tomatoes and pepper and cook for 5 minutes to soften them. Stir in the courgettes, balsamic vinegar, capers, chopped basil and seasoning and leave to simmer.

3 After 10 minutes, stir well, add the salmon fillets then cover and cook gently for about 7 minutes until the salmon is cooked. If it is a little undercooked, leave in the pan for a few minutes to continue cooking in the residual heat.

4 Scatter with the basil leaves and serve.

(V) Try this To make a lovely vegetarian supper, omit the salmon, swap the stock for a vegetable one and serve the sauce with 40 g (1½ oz) dried pasta per person, cooked according to packet instructions, for 4 *ProPoints* values per serving.

Prawns with oyster sauce and greens

ProPoints values per recipe 11
Takes 20 mins

Serves 4

2 tablespoons cornflour

60 ml (2 fl oz) oyster sauce

3 x 5 cm (2 inch) slices fresh root ginger, sliced thinly then cut into matchsticks

2 garlic cloves, sliced

200 g (7 oz) tenderstem broccoli, stems peeled (see Cook's tip)

225 g can water chestnuts, drained

150 g (5½ oz) sugarsnap peas

4 spring onions, cut into lengths

300 g (10½ oz) raw tiger prawns, thawed if frozen

90 g (3½ oz) baby pak choi, halved

Water chestnuts add a lovely crunchy texture to this stir fry. Serve with 60 g (2 oz) dried brown rice per person, cooked according to packet instructions, for an extra 6 **ProPoints** values per serving.

1 Mix together the cornflour and oyster sauce with 225 ml (8 fl oz) water and the ginger and garlic. Pour into a large wok and cook over a medium heat, stirring until thickened.

2 Add the broccoli and water chestnuts to the wok and cook for 3 minutes. Stir in the sugarsnap peas and spring onions and cook for a further 3 minutes.

3 Add the prawns and pak choi and stir until the prawns turn pink but take care not to overcook or the prawns will toughen and the pak choi will wilt. Serve immediately.

Cook's tip The best way to peel the tenderstem broccoli is to use a vegetable peeler.

Herby fish crumble

ProPoints values per recipe 28
25 mins prep, 15 mins cooking

Serves 4

2 leeks, washed, trimmed and sliced thinly

400 ml (14 fl oz) skimmed milk

1 tablespoon English mustard

150 g (5½ oz) button mushrooms

200 g (7 oz) skinless smoked haddock

200 g (7 oz) skinless cod loin

200 g (7 oz) low fat soft cheese

1 tablespoon cornflour

100 g (3½ oz) frozen peas

100 g (3½ oz) cherry tomatoes, halved

salt and freshly ground black pepper

For the crumble topping

1 medium slice stale wholemeal bread

15 g (½ oz) plain flour

½ teaspoon mixed dried herbs

15 g (½ oz) low fat spread

The crumble works best with bread that is a few days old. If your bread is fresh, leave it out to allow it to dry a little before using. Serve with broccoli or a zero **ProPoints** value green salad, for no extra **ProPoints** values per serving.

1 Put the leeks, milk, mustard and mushrooms in a flameproof and ovenproof casserole dish. Heat gently for 15 minutes until the leeks are soft.

2 Preheat the oven to Gas Mark 6/200°C/fan oven 180°C. To make the crumble topping, tear the bread, put it in a food processor and whizz to make crumbs. Put the crumbs in a bowl and add the flour, dried herbs and low fat spread with a little seasoning then lightly mix together to make the crumble topping. Cut the fish into large chunks.

3 Take the leeks off the heat and beat in the soft cheese and cornflour. Stir in the peas, add the chunks of fish and scatter over the cherry tomatoes followed by the herby crumbs.

4 Bake in the oven for 15 minutes until the crumbs are crisp and the fish is just cooked.

Crab and rocket linguine

ProPoints values per recipe 9
Takes 10 mins

Serves 1

75 g (2¾ oz) dried linguine, snapped
   in half
1 spring onion, chopped finely
½ red chilli, chopped finely
1 garlic clove, chopped finely
grated zest and juice of ½ a lime
170 g can white crabmeat in brine,
   drained
a handful of rocket leaves
salt and freshly ground black pepper

Spoil yourself with this speedy but incredibly tasty pasta dish.

1 Bring a large pan of water to the boil, add the linguine, return to the boil, and cook for 5 minutes. Drain but reserve a mugful of the pasta water.

2 Return the pasta to the pan then toss really well with the spring onion, chilli, garlic and lime zest adding a little of the pasta water to loosen the texture. Gently toss in the crab, add the lime juice and season. Serve topped with the rocket leaves.

Try this You could also add 50 g (1¾ oz) frozen peas for 11 **ProPoints** values per serving. Add in step 1, after the pasta has cooked for 5 minutes, then return to the boil and cook for 2 minutes more. Follow the remaining instructions.

Baked sea bass with potatoes and onions

ProPoints values per recipe 13
20 mins prep, 42 mins cooking

Serves 2

¼ **kettleful of boiling water**

1 **large** onion**, halved and sliced thinly**

250 g (9 oz) potatoes**, scrubbed and**
  sliced thinly

½ **teaspoon dried oregano, plus a**
  good pinch

2 tomatoes**, sliced**

2 garlic cloves**, 1 sliced and 1 chopped**
  finely

1 **lemon**

calorie controlled cooking spray

1 **teaspoon extra virgin olive oil**

2 x 125 g (4½ oz) sea bass **fillets**

salt and freshly ground black pepper

This sea bass recipe tastes surprisingly special for hardly any effort.

1 Put the onion in a large bowl. Pour over boiling water to cover and set aside for about 15 minutes to soften.

2 Preheat the oven to Gas Mark 7/220°C/fan oven 200°C. Drain the onion, return to the bowl then toss with the potato slices, the oregano, the tomatoes, sliced garlic, the grated zest from half of the lemon and a little seasoning. Line a baking tray with a large sheet of foil and spray with the cooking spray. Spread out the potato mixture on top then spray with a little more cooking spray and bake for 30 minutes.

3 To make the dressing, squeeze the juice from the remaining lemon half into a bowl. Mix in the chopped garlic, the pinch of oregano, olive oil and seasoning and 1 tablespoon of water then set aside. Cut four slices from the remaining lemon half.

4 Remove the potatoes from the oven, lay the fish, skin side up, on top of the potatoes, and top with the lemon slices. Season and spray with the cooking spray. Return to the oven for 10–12 minutes until the potatoes are tender and golden and the fish is cooked. Spoon over the dressing to serve.

Smoky jackets

ProPoints values per recipe 32
15 mins prep, 1 hr 15 mins cooking

Serves 4

4 x 225 g (8 oz) **baking** potatoes

calorie controlled cooking spray

198 g **can** sweetcorn**, drained**

3 spring onions**, sliced finely**

150 g (5½ oz) **skinned** smoked haddock**,**
  undyed, cut into chunks

8 cherry tomatoes**, quartered**

40 g (1½ oz) **half fat Cheddar cheese,**
  grated

salt and freshly ground black pepper

These jacket potatoes are ideal for a family Saturday lunch. The puréed sweetcorn makes them deliciously creamy.

1 Preheat the oven to Gas Mark 6/200°C/fan oven 180°C. Place the potatoes on a baking sheet, spray with the cooking spray and bake for 1 hour. Meanwhile, tip the sweetcorn into a bowl and blitz with a hand blender, or in a food processor, to make a purée.

2 Take the potatoes from the oven and cut in half. Carefully scoop the flesh into a bowl, keeping a rim of potato still round the shells so that they hold their shape. Mash the potato with the puréed corn and seasoning then stir in the onions, haddock and tomatoes.

3 Pile the mixture back into the shells, sprinkle with the cheese and bake for 15 minutes.

Try this Instead of smoked haddock, try a 185 g can of tuna chunks in brine, drained, for the same *ProPoints* values per serving.

Hot 'n' sour prawn soup

ProPoints values per recipe 10
15 mins prep, 20 mins cooking

Serves 4

220 g pack frozen raw peeled king
  prawns, thawed

1.5 litres (2¾ pints) fish stock

strips of zest from 1 lime (see Cook's tip)

6 x 5 cm (2 inch) slices fresh root ginger

1 blade lemongrass, halved and bruised
  (see Cook's tip)

2 red chillies, 1 halved and 1 de-seeded
  and chopped finely

½ orange pepper, de-seeded and cut
  into matchstick strips

2 garlic cloves, sliced

3 spring onions, cut into lengths

50 g (1¾ oz) dried thin rice noodles

1 tablespoon fish sauce

75 g (2¾ oz) beansprouts

2 tablespoons chopped fresh coriander

This Asian style noodle broth has plenty of heat and flavour from the chilli, lime and ginger.

1 Cut the prawns in half lengthways then set aside.

2 Pour the stock into a large lidded saucepan. Add the lime zest to the pan with the ginger, lemongrass and halved chilli and bring to the boil. Reduce the heat then cover and simmer for 15 minutes to release the flavours into the stock. Remove the flavourings with a slotted spoon and discard.

3 Add the pepper, chilli, garlic and spring onions to the stock and cook for 5 minutes. Snap the noodles in half, add to the pan and cook for a couple of minutes to soften them.

4 Add the prawns, fish sauce, beansprouts and coriander and allow to cook for a few seconds until the prawns turn pink and curl. Serve immediately.

Cook's tips To release the aromatic oils and flavour of lemongrass, hit it firmly with either a rolling pin or the bottom of a saucepan to flatten it.
  To make lime zest strips, use a vegetable peeler.

Smoked salmon tortilla

ProPoints values per recipe 20
Takes 20 mins

Serves 4

300 g (10½ oz) large new potatoes, sliced

a kettleful of boiling water

2 courgettes, sliced

5 eggs

125 g (4½ oz) smoked salmon trimmings

1 tablespoon chopped fresh dill, plus
  extra to serve

1 spring onion, chopped finely

calorie controlled cooking spray

freshly ground black pepper

A great dish for a brunch, lunch or picnic. Serve warm or cold with a zero **ProPoints** value tomato salad.

1 Put the potato slices in a deep, large, lidded, non stick frying pan and pour over the boiling water. Bring to the boil then cover and simmer for about 5 minutes. Add the courgettes then cook for 3 minutes more until the potatoes are just tender when pierced with a knife. Drain and set aside.

2 Meanwhile, in a large bowl, beat the eggs and add the salmon, dill, and spring onion with plenty of black pepper. Stir in the potato and courgette slices and toss well.

3 Heat the frying pan and spray with the cooking spray. Add the egg and potato mixture. Cover and cook gently for 5 minutes until set on the base. Preheat the grill to a high temperature. Cook under the grill for a few minutes to set the top then scatter over the extra dill and serve.

Lemony fish with herby oven chips

ProPoints values per recipe 14

Takes 35 mins

Serves 2

calorie controlled cooking spray

300 g (10½ oz) potatoes**, scrubbed and cut into chunky chips**

1½ teaspoons finely chopped fresh rosemary

grated zest of ½ a lemon

2 tablespoons fresh breadcrumbs

2 x 125 g (4½ oz) chunky cod loin **pieces**

2 teaspoons green pesto

2 tomatoes**, halved**

salt and freshly ground black pepper

2 lemon wedges, to serve

Here's a great twist on the traditional fish and chips. Instead of a batter coating, the fish is flavoured with pesto and lemony crumbs. Serve with 80 g (3 oz) **peas** for an extra 2 **ProPoints** values per person or with a zero **ProPoints** value **salad**.

1 Preheat the oven to Gas Mark 7/220°C/fan oven 200°C. Spray a large non stick baking sheet with the cooking spray and scatter over the potatoes, spacing them apart. Sprinkle over a teaspoon of the rosemary with some black pepper. Spray again with the cooking spray and bake for 10 minutes. Remove from the oven, turn over the chips and cook for about 8 minutes longer until they start to brown.

2 Meanwhile, mix the lemon zest and remaining rosemary with the breadcrumbs and some seasoning. Smear the whole fish with the pesto then scatter the crumbs all over.

3 Put on the baking tray with the chips and tomatoes. Cook for about 8 minutes until just cooked. Serve with the lemon wedges.

Poached fish with Oriental broth

ProPoints values per recipe 10
Takes 25 mins

Serves 2

500 ml (18 fl oz) chicken stock
1 tablespoon soy sauce
1 tablespoon rice wine vinegar
½ cm (¼ inch) fresh root ginger, sliced
   thinly and cut into matchsticks
2 large garlic cloves, shredded or
   chopped finely
2 x 175 g (6 oz) white skinned plaice fillets
50 g (1¾ oz) frozen soya beans
100 g (3½ oz) broccoli florets, cut
   into small pieces
1 large carrot, peeled and grated coarsely
1 Chinese leaf, shredded
2 spring onions, sliced at an angle

This is also delicious with 60 g (2 oz) dried rice per person, cooked according to packet instructions, for an extra 6 **ProPoints** values.

1 Pour the stock into a deep, lidded, non stick frying pan with the soy sauce and vinegar. Add the ginger and garlic. Heat until just bubbling then reduce the heat, cover and simmer for 5 minutes.
2 Meanwhile, snip each plaice fillet in half lengthways with scissors – you will see the natural divide. Roll up from the thick end, skin side in. Put in the pan with the stock mixture, cover and cook gently for 3 minutes. Lift out with a slotted spoon and set aside.
3 Add the soya beans to the pan with the broccoli and carrot then cook, covered, for 4 minutes. Stir in the Chinese leaf and spring onions, return the fish to the pan and cook for 1 minute more. Serve immediately in shallow bowls.

Try this For a hotter version, add some sliced fresh chilli to the broth at the start of cooking, or stir in some fragrant fresh coriander at the end, for no extra **ProPoints** values.

Tuna and bean enchiladas

ProPoints values per recipe 39
20 mins prep, 40 mins cooking

Serves 4

420 g can red kidney beans in water,
   drained
185 g can tuna in brine, drained
300 g jar hot salsa
198 g can naturally sweet sweetcorn,
   drained
2 spring onions, chopped finely
20 g pack fresh coriander, chopped
8 cherry tomatoes, quartered
4 soft flour tortillas
100 g (3½ oz) fat free plain fromage frais
50 g (1¾ oz) half fat Cheddar cheese,
   grated finely
2 tablespoons skimmed milk
¼ teaspoon ground coriander
a good pinch of ground cumin

These enchiladas make a great meal for all the family. Serve with a crunchy salad of onion, shredded white cabbage and carrot, for no extra **ProPoints** values per serving.

1 Preheat the oven to Gas Mark 5/190°C/fan oven 170°C. Put the beans in a bowl and crush them lightly. Flake the tuna and add to the bowl, then stir in the salsa, sweetcorn, spring onions, all but 1 tablespoon of the fresh coriander and tomatoes.
2 Warm the tortillas on a plate in the microwave, or over a gas flame in a frying pan to soften them a little, then cut in half with scissors. Roll up each one with an eighth of the filling inside. Put in pairs in a large, shallow ovenproof dish.
3 In a bowl, mix the fromage frais with the cheese and skimmed milk, ground coriander and remaining fresh coriander, and cumin. Spread this mixture over the tortillas to cover them. Bake in the oven for 30–40 minutes until heated through.

Seafood oven risotto

ProPoints values per recipe 35
10 mins prep, 23 mins cooking
Serves 4

a good pinch of saffron threads
700 ml (1¼ pints) chicken stock
calorie controlled cooking spray
40 g (1½ oz) chorizo, skinned and chopped finely
1 large onion, **chopped finely**
2 garlic cloves, **chopped**
225 g (8 oz) dried risotto rice
1 tablespoon white wine vinegar
1 large yellow pepper, **chopped**
400 g can cherry tomatoes **in rich tomato juice**
400 g pack frozen raw fruits de mer, **just thawed**
100 g (3½ oz) frozen petits pois
3 tablespoons chopped fresh parsley
salt and freshly ground black pepper

A cross between a paella and a risotto, this tasty supper is so easy. It's the perfect treat for a Saturday night. You can serve on its own, or with a leafy salad with rocket and endive, for no additional **ProPoints** values.

1 Preheat the oven to Gas Mark 6/200°C/fan oven 180°C. Add the saffron to the stock and stir.

2 Heat a large, lidded, flameproof and ovenproof pan and spray with the cooking spray. Add the chorizo, onion and garlic then cover and cook gently for about a minute to soften the onion. Stir in the rice, mix well then add the white wine vinegar and let it cook gently for a few seconds.

3 Pour in the saffron stock and chopped pepper, then add the cherry tomatoes. Stir gently so that you don't crush them. Bring to the boil then cover and bake in the oven for 18 minutes until the rice is cooked.

4 Stir the frozen seafood, petits pois and parsley into the rice with a little seasoning. Cover and return to the oven for 5 minutes more until the prawns turn from grey to pink.

Try this Chorizo is a spicy Spanish sausage, flavoured with paprika. A little goes a long way, but if you want a deeper flavour, add ¼ teaspoon smoked paprika to the risotto when stirring the rice into the pan, for no extra **ProPoints** values.

Vegetarian meals

With their exciting flavours and interesting textures, these sensational veggie meals are a great choice for family and friends and are sure to fill everyone up.

Ruby beetroot risotto

6
ProPoints value

ProPoints values per recipe 24

Takes 35 mins

 Serves 4

calorie controlled cooking spray

2 red onions, chopped finely

2 garlic cloves, chopped

175 g (6 oz) dried risotto rice

150 ml (5 fl oz) dry white wine

up to 1 litre (1¾ pints) hot vegetable stock

½ teaspoon hot horseradish

75 g (2¾ oz) low fat soft cheese

300 g pack fresh cooked beetroot, chopped

1 tablespoon chopped fresh dill, plus extra to garnish

salt and freshly ground black pepper

This brightly coloured risotto is delicious accompanied by a salad of rocket, watercress and baby spinach with some chopped red onion and a few orange slices.

1 Heat a large, deep, non stick frying pan or saucepan. Spray with the cooking spray and fry the onions and garlic for 5 minutes, stirring frequently, until softened. Tip in the rice and stir over the heat until you hear it start to crackle – about a minute or two.

2 Pour in the wine then simmer to almost nothing to evaporate the alcohol but leave the flavour of the wine.

3 Pour about a quarter of the stock into the pan with some seasoning. Cook gently, stirring frequently, for about 15 minutes. Top up with the stock as it gets absorbed. As the rice starts to cook, you won't need to stir it quite so much. Meanwhile, mix the horseradish into the soft cheese.

4 Add the beetroot to the rice and stir well. Taste and, if necessary, cook for 5 minutes more. The rice should have quite a moist, creamy consistency, but not be mushy.

5 Allow to rest for 5 minutes then stir in the dill. Serve with the horseradish and cheese mixture on the side or mixed in, and topped with a little extra dill.

Honeyed vegetable tagine

ProPoints values per recipe 24

25 mins prep, 25 mins cooking

V   **Serves 4**

calorie controlled cooking spray

1 large onion, chopped finely

4 garlic cloves, chopped

400 g can chopped tomatoes

500 ml (18 fl oz) vegetable stock

1 tablespoon hot chilli powder

1 tablespoon ground cumin

500 g (1 lb 2 oz) cauliflower florets

300 g (10½ oz) sweet potato, cubed

400 g (14 oz) carrots, peeled and
    sliced thickly

1 green pepper, de-seeded and cubed

100 g (3½ oz) pitted prunes

1 tablespoon clear honey

410 g can chick peas in water, drained

salt and freshly ground black pepper

Dried prunes provide a sweet, rich contrast to the hot spices and nutty chick peas in this stew. Serve with 60 g (2 oz) dried couscous per person, cooked according to packet instructions, for an extra 6 *ProPoints* values per serving.

1 Heat a large, deep, lidded, non stick frying pan. Spray with the cooking spray then fry the onion and garlic for 5 minutes, stirring frequently. Add the tomatoes and stock then stir in the chilli powder and cumin. Cover and simmer for 10 minutes.

2 Stir in the cauliflower, sweet potato, carrots, green pepper and prunes. Drizzle in the honey and season to taste. Cover and simmer for 20 minutes until the vegetables are almost tender. Add the chick peas and simmer for a further 5 minutes. Serve immediately.

Cheat's veggie moussaka

ProPoints values per recipe 21
20 mins prep, 45 mins cooking
V   **Serves 6**

calorie controlled cooking spray
2 large onions, halved and sliced
3 garlic cloves, chopped
400 g can chopped tomatoes
2 tablespoons tomato purée
400 ml (14 fl oz) vegetable stock
½ teaspoon ground cinnamon
3 bay leaves
½ teaspoon dried oregano
200 g (7 oz) potatoes, peeled, halved
    and sliced
1 large aubergine, halved and sliced
350 g pack Quorn mince
250 g (9 oz) low fat fromage frais
1 egg
25 g (1 oz) feta light, crumbled
4 tomatoes, sliced
salt and freshly ground black pepper

A zero **ProPoints** value tomato, onion and rocket salad makes a refreshing accompaniment for this delicious moussaka.

1 Preheat the oven to Gas Mark 4/180°C/fan oven 160°C. Heat a lidded flameproof and ovenproof dish, spray with the cooking spray then add the onions and garlic. Stir well then cover and cook for just under 10 minutes, stirring occasionally and adding a splash of water if they start to stick.

2 Add the canned tomatoes, purée and stock to the dish then stir in the cinnamon, bay leaves and oregano. Stir well then add the potato and aubergine slices.

3 Cover and leave to simmer for 20 minutes until the aubergine is soft and the potatoes are tender. Remove from the heat and stir in the Quorn.

4 Beat the fromage frais with the egg and the feta cheese and spread over the Quorn mixture. Arrange the fresh tomato slices on top and season. Bake in the oven for 25 minutes until the topping is set.

Cook's tip Quorn is made using a member of the mushroom family. It's naturally low in fat but high in protein and fibre.

Zesty tofu noodles

ProPoints values per recipe 29
Takes 25 mins
Ⓥ
Serves 4

grated zest and juice of 1 lime
1 tablespoon soy sauce
2 tablespoons sweet chilli sauce
calorie controlled cooking spray
4 spring onions, sliced
1 orange or red pepper, quartered,
    de-seeded and sliced thinly
225 g can bamboo shoots in water, drained
2 garlic cloves, chopped
1 red chilli, de-seeded and chopped
160 g (5¾ oz) marinated tofu pieces
2 x 150 g packs straight to wok rice
    ribbon noodles
200 g (7 oz) beansprouts
1 tablespoon chopped roasted peanuts
4 tablespoons chopped fresh coriander
1 egg, beaten

This wok dish uses marinated tofu rather than the plain type which many people find too bland.

1 In a bowl, mix the lime zest and juice with the soy sauce, chilli sauce and 3 tablespoons of water.
2 Heat a non stick wok, spray with the cooking spray and add the spring onions, pepper, bamboo shoots, garlic and chilli. Stir fry for 5 minutes until the vegetables begin to soften.
3 Pour the lime mixture into the pan then add the tofu, noodles and beansprouts and stir well over the heat to mix everything together. Cook until everything is piping hot, about 3–5 minutes, and then take the pan off the heat and toss in the peanuts, coriander and beaten egg. The egg will cook instantly as it gets tossed into the hot noodles. Serve immediately.

Moroccan eggs

ProPoints values per recipe 9
Takes 30 mins
Ⓥ
Serves 2

calorie controlled cooking spray
1 onion, halved and sliced thinly
2 garlic cloves, sliced
1½ teaspoons rose harissa paste
½ teaspoon ground coriander
300 ml (10 fl oz) vegetable stock
400 g can cherry tomatoes in rich
    tomato juice
2 courgettes, diced finely
220 g can chick peas in water, drained
2 tablespoons chopped fresh coriander
2 eggs

Serve with a medium slice of unbuttered wholewheat toast per person, for an extra 2 **ProPoints** values per serving.

1 Heat a lidded non stick frying pan, spray with the cooking spray and add the onion and garlic. Fry them, stirring constantly, until starting to soften. Add the harissa paste and ground coriander, stir well then pour in the vegetable stock. Cover and simmer for 5 minutes.
2 Add the tomatoes and courgettes and then cook gently for 10 minutes until the courgettes are tender. Stir in the chick peas and coriander then make two hollows in the mixture and break in the eggs. Cover and cook for 2 minutes then allow to settle for a further 2 minutes before serving.

Cook's tip If you can't find a 220 g can of chick peas, measure out 130 g (4½ oz) from a larger can.

Vegetable dhansak

ProPoints values per recipe 21
20 mins prep, 25 mins cooking

 V ✿   **Serves 4**

150 g (5½ oz) dried split red lentils

2.5 cm (1 inch) fresh root ginger, sliced thinly and cut into matchsticks

4 garlic cloves, sliced

2 large onions, chopped roughly

2 green chillies, sliced (de-seeded if preferred)

1 cinnamon stick

2 bay leaves

1 aubergine, cut into large chunks

300 g (10½ oz) potatoes, peeled and cut into cubes

1 teaspoon ground cumin

2 teaspoons ground coriander

½ teaspoon ground turmeric

2 tablespoons tomato purée

1 vegetable stock cube

150 g (5½ oz) young spinach leaves

This lentil curry is delicious with a tablespoon of mango chutney and a Weight Watchers mini plain naan per person for an extra 4 **ProPoints** values per serving or 60 g (2 oz) dried brown basmati rice, cooked according to packet instructions, for an extra 6 **ProPoints** values per serving.

1 Add the lentils to a large lidded pan with the ginger, garlic, onions, chillies, cinnamon stick, bay leaves and aubergine. Pour over 1 litre (1¾ pints) cold water and bring to the boil. Cover and leave to simmer for 10 minutes.

2 Remove the pan from the heat and stir in the potatoes, spices, tomato purée and stock cube. Return to the heat, cover again and leave to cook for a further 15 minutes until the vegetables are tender and the lentils are pulpy.

3 Turn off the heat and stir in the spinach leaves, allowing them to wilt in the heat – there is no need to cook them. Season to taste.

Cook's tip Salt or salty ingredients such as a stock cube shouldn't be added to lentils or dried beans at the beginning of cooking since they can make them tough.

Cheesy spinach pudding

ProPoints values per recipe 21
20 mins prep, 50 mins cooking

(V)   **Makes 4**

450 g bag ready washed spinach
a kettleful of boiling water
75 g (2¾ oz) wholemeal bread
3 eggs
150 ml (5 fl oz) skimmed milk
200 g (7 oz) low fat cottage cheese
1 tablespoon English mustard
75 g (2¾ oz) reduced fat Cheddar
cheese, grated
calorie controlled cooking spray
12 cherry tomatoes**, halved**
salt and freshly ground black pepper

This is delicious with a zero *ProPoints* value salad on the side.

1 Preheat the oven to Gas Mark 6/200°C/fan oven 180°C. Put the spinach in a colander and pour over all the boiling water to wilt it. When cool, drain and squeeze out as much of the water as you can.
2 Put the bread in a food processor then add the eggs, milk, cottage cheese, mustard and seasoning. Whizz to mix everything together then add the spinach and 25 g (1 oz) of the cheese and whizz together briefly.
3 Spray a 1 litre (1¾ pint) dish with the cooking spray. Pour in the spinach mixture and scatter with the tomatoes and remaining cheese. Bake for 45–50 minutes or until puffed up and golden.

Cook's tip Pre-washed spinach can be cooked in its packaging in the microwave on high for a few minutes.

Gardener's pie

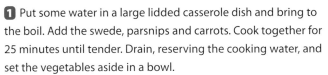

ProPoints values per recipe 21
15 mins prep, 50 mins cooking

(V) ❄   **Serves 6**

800 g (1 lb 11 oz) swede**, peeled and**
cubed
450 g (1 lb) parsnips**, peeled and chopped**
450 g (1 lb) carrots**, peeled and chopped**
2 large onions**, chopped**
2 garlic cloves**, chopped**
3 celery **sticks, sliced**
1 teaspoon mixed dried herbs
2 teaspoons yeast extract
1 vegetable stock cube
410 g can green lentils **in water, drained**
a pinch of freshly grated nutmeg
50 g (1¾ oz) half fat Cheddar cheese,
grated
freshly ground black pepper

Here's a delicious veggie version of Shepherd's pie, topped with a root vegetable mash rather than the more usual potato one.

1 Put some water in a large lidded casserole dish and bring to the boil. Add the swede, parsnips and carrots. Cook together for 25 minutes until tender. Drain, reserving the cooking water, and set the vegetables aside in a bowl.
2 Rinse the dish and then return the cooking liquid, making it up to 450 ml (16 fl oz) with water. Add the onions, garlic, celery, mixed herbs, yeast extract and stock cube. Cover and cook for 20 minutes until tender. Add the green lentils and cook for a few minutes more.
3 Preheat the grill to high. Meanwhile, mash the swede mixture with the nutmeg and black pepper.
4 When the lentil mixture is ready, spoon the mash on top and roughly spread it over to cover. Scatter over the cheese and put under the grill until golden and bubbling then serve.

South African stuffed squash

ProPoints values per recipe 18

15 mins prep, 1½ hrs cooking

 V

Serves 4

2 small **butternut squash, halved
    lengthways and seeds removed**
calorie controlled cooking spray
3 tablespoons tomato purée
**2 teaspoons hot curry paste, such as
    rogan josh**
½ teaspoon ground mixed spice
½ teaspoon dried mixed herbs
2 tablespoons sultanas
1 tablespoon mango chutney
200 ml (7 fl oz) vegetable stock
350 g pack Quorn mince
4 bay leaves
freshly ground black pepper

Based on the sweet and spicy flavours of the South African national dish called 'bobotie', this recipe uses Quorn mince rather than meat. Serve with 60 g (2 oz) dried rice, boiled with a little stock, turmeric and fresh coriander, for an extra 6 *ProPoints* values per person.

1 Preheat the oven to Gas Mark 6/200°C/fan oven 180°C. Put the squash halves on a baking tray, cut side up and spray with the cooking spray. Cover with foil and roast for 30 minutes.

2 Meanwhile, mix the tomato purée, curry paste, mixed spice, mixed herbs, sultanas and chutney in a bowl with the vegetable stock. Stir in the Quorn and season with black pepper.

3 Remove the squash from the oven and spoon the spicy mixture into their hollows. Top each one with a bay leaf. Cover with foil and bake in the oven for 1 hour or until the squash are tender. Remove the bay leaves and serve.

Try this You can replace the Quorn mince with 350 g (12 oz) extra lean beef mince for 6 *ProPoints* values per serving. Add it in step 2, instead of the Quorn, and follow the instructions from there. There is no need to pre-fry the mince.

Carrot, butterbean and tarragon soup

ProPoints values per recipe 7

15 mins prep, 30 mins cooking

 V ❄

Serves 4

2 **garlic cloves, chopped**
300 g (10½ oz) leeks**, sliced**
1 onion**, chopped finely**
700 g (1 lb 9 oz) carrots**, peeled
    and chopped**
1.4 litres (2½ pints) vegetable stock
1 tablespoon chopped fresh tarragon
  or 2 teaspoons dried tarragon
410 g can butterbeans **in water, drained**
salt and freshly ground black pepper

Soup makes a very satisfying lunch and freezes well too. Enjoy a bowl with a medium slice of crusty wholemeal bread per person for an extra 2 *ProPoints* values per serving.

1 Put the garlic, vegetables, stock and tarragon into a large lidded saucepan and bring to the boil. Cover and leave to simmer for 30 minutes until the vegetables are tender.

2 Purée half of the soup only with a hand held blender to thicken it but still retain some of the texture. Then stir in the butterbeans. Heat through then season to taste.

Try this For a spicy version, add ground coriander and cumin and replace the tarragon with fresh coriander for the same *ProPoints* values per person.

Mixed bean goulash

calorie controlled cooking spray

5 shallots, peeled and halved

1 large green pepper, de-seeded
　and sliced

¼ teaspoon caraway seeds

1 teaspoon fresh thyme leaves

1 teaspoon paprika

400 g can chopped tomatoes

1–2 teaspoons tomato purée

400 ml (14 fl oz) vegetable stock

1 celery stick, sliced

1 carrot, peeled and sliced

3 garlic cloves, crushed finely

420 g can mixed bean salad in water,
　drained

150 g pot low fat plain yogurt

salt and freshly ground black pepper

The flavours in this veggie goulash work very well with ready cooked beans. Serve with a 30 g (1¼ oz) slice of warm, crusty bread per person, for an extra 2 **ProPoints** values per serving.

1 Heat a deep, lidded, non stick frying pan and spray with the cooking spray. Add the shallots then cook, cut side down, to brown them. Add the pepper then cover the pan and cook for about 3 minutes to soften them. Tip in the caraway seeds and stir well.

2 Stir in the thyme, paprika, tomatoes, tomato purée and stock. Add the celery, carrot and two-thirds of the garlic and stir well. Cover and cook for 20 minutes until the vegetables are tender. Stir in the beans and heat through. Season to taste if necessary.

3 Meanwhile, mix the yogurt with the remaining garlic and season to taste. Serve the goulash with the yogurt and an extra sprinkle of paprika if you like.

Try this For a pork goulash, thickly slice 400 g (14 oz) lean pork tenderloin. Add in step 2 and then follow the cooking instructions. The **ProPoints** values per serving will be 6.

Summer salsa spaghetti

100 g (3½ oz) dried spaghetti

2 large ripe tomatoes, chopped finely

1 red onion, chopped very finely

2 tablespoons small capers in brine,
　drained

40 g (1½ oz) pimiento stuffed olives,
　halved

½ teaspoon red chilli, chopped finely

grated zest and juice of ½ a lemon,
　to taste

3 tablespoons shredded fresh basil

salt and freshly ground black pepper

This toss-and-serve pasta dish has a no-cook dressing that is packed full of Mediterranean flavours. Make sure you use really ripe tomatoes for the best colour and taste.

1 Bring a large pan of water to the boil, snap the spaghetti in half, add to the pan and cook according to the packet instructions until al dente, about 9 minutes.

2 Meanwhile, mix the tomatoes with the onion, capers, olives, chilli, lemon zest and basil.

3 Drain the pasta then tip the tomato mixture into the pan and toss well. Season and drizzle over the lemon juice, to taste. Serve immediately.

Cook's tip As a change from lemon, try balsamic vinegar. You will need about 1 teaspoon to replace the juice and zest for the same **ProPoints** values per serving.

Delicious desserts

Find the perfect way to end to your meal with these easy ideas. Treat yourself to a slice of tart or a piece of cake. Or perhaps some meringue or lemon surprise?

Filo plum tart

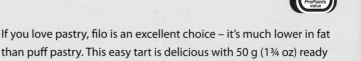

ProPoints values per recipe 18

15 mins prep + cooling, 30 mins baking

 Makes 6 slices

calorie controlled cooking spray

3 x 45 g (1½ oz) large sheets of filo pastry

2 tablespoons ground almonds

12 small, firm plums, halved and stoned

¼ teaspoon ground cinnamon

2 tablespoons caster sugar

1 teaspoon icing sugar, for dusting

If you love pastry, filo is an excellent choice – it's much lower in fat than puff pastry. This easy tart is delicious with 50 g (1¾ oz) ready to eat low fat custard per person for an extra 1 *ProPoints* value per serving, or a 60 g (2 oz) scoop of low fat ice cream per person, for an extra 2 *ProPoints* values per serving.

1 Preheat the oven to Gas Mark 6/200˚C/fan oven 180˚C. Spray a small Swiss roll tin with a little cooking spray and line with a sheet of filo pastry, trimming it to fit with scissors.

2 Place the pastry trimmings on top, then cover with the next layer of pastry, putting the trimmings between the whole sheets and spraying as you go, ending with a whole sheet of filo.

3 Scatter the filo with the ground almonds then arrange the plums on top. Mix the cinnamon into the sugar and sprinkle over the plums. Bake for 25–30 minutes until the pastry is golden and the plums are tender. Leave to cool before slicing and serving, with the icing sugar dusted over the top using a small sieve.

Try this If you slice the plums into quarters, you can bake the tart for less time. After 20 minutes, the plums will be tender and ready to eat.

Sponge pudding with apricot sauce

ProPoints values per recipe 31
15 mins prep, 30 mins baking
                                    Serves 6

calorie controlled cooking spray
220 g can apricots in natural juice
3 eggs, **separated**
grated zest and juice of 1 small orange
3 tablespoons thick set honey
75 g (2¾ oz) mixed dried fruit
75 g (2¾ oz) self-raising wholemeal flour
½ teaspoon ground mixed spice

It might seem impossible to make a sponge pudding without butter or low fat spread, but this is lovely without adding either.

1 Preheat the oven to Gas Mark 5/190°C/fan oven 170°C. Lightly spray a 1.2 litre (2 pint) pudding basin with the cooking spray and line the base with baking parchment.

2 Whizz the apricots and juice in a food processor, or with a hand held blender, until smooth, then put 4 tablespoons of the mixture into the pudding basin and swirl it up the sides.

3 Using an electric whisk, beat the egg yolks, orange zest and honey until pale and creamy. Mix together the dried fruit, flour and mixed spice then gently fold into the egg yolk mixture, followed by the orange juice.

4 Whisk the egg whites with an electric whisk in a clean, grease-free bowl until stiff and then fold into the egg yolk mixture. Pour the mixture into the basin then bake for 25–30 minutes until firm and springy.

5 Turn out and serve sliced with the remaining apricot purée.

Raspberry baked peaches

ProPoints values per recipe 6
15 mins prep + cooling, 20 mins baking
                                    Serves 4

4 firm, ripe peaches, **halved and stoned**
**100 g Weight Watchers raspberry
layered summer fruits fromage frais**
**100 g Weight Watchers peach layered
summer fruits fromage frais**
100 g (3½ oz) frozen raspberries
2 tablespoons caster sugar

When peaches and nectarines are ripe and in season, this makes a lovely summer dessert that's special enough for entertaining friends al fresco.

1 Preheat the oven to Gas Mark 5/190°C/fan oven 170°C. Arrange the peaches in a large, shallow ovenproof dish.

2 Spoon both flavours of the fromage frais into a bowl and swirl them together so the colours marble. Spoon into the hollows left by the peach stones and scatter with the raspberries and sugar.

3 Bake for 20 minutes until the peaches are tender. Cool for 5–10 minutes before serving.

Crumbly baked apples

ProPoints values per recipe 29
15 mins prep, 1 hour 10 mins baking
Ⓥ   **Serves 4**

4 even sized Bramley apples
12 soft pitted dried dates
150 ml (5 fl oz) unsweetened apple juice
25 g (1 oz) low fat spread
40 g (1½ oz) plain flour
15 g (½ oz) porridge oats
¼ teaspoon ground cinnamon
50 g (1¾ oz) demerara sugar

Serve with 1 tablespoon of **0% fat Greek yogurt** per person, for an additional 1 **ProPoints** value per serving, or 50 g (1¾ oz) of ready to eat low fat custard per person, for an extra 1 **ProPoints** value per serving.

1 Preheat the oven to Gas Mark 6/200°C/fan oven 180°C. Carefully cut the core from each apple and cut round the middle into the skin to score them so they don't split in the oven.

2 Put the apples in a baking dish so they fit quite snugly then push three dates into the hollows left by the cores. Pour over the apple juice and bake in the oven for 40 minutes until the apples are almost tender.

3 Meanwhile, rub the low fat spread with the flour, oats, cinnamon and sugar to make a clumpy crumble mixture.

4 Remove the apples from the oven, slip the top skin from each apple and discard then press the crumble mixture on to the exposed flesh. Return to the oven for 30 minutes until the apples are fully cooked and the crumble is golden.

Orange fluff

ProPoints values per recipe 17
Takes 10 mins + 4 hrs chilling
                                    Serves 6

135 g packet orange jelly
298 g can mandarin oranges **in juice**
170 g can light evaporated milk

Everyone will love this simple but tasty family dessert.

1 Break the jelly into a jug. Add 100ml (3½ fl oz) water then microwave on high for about 1 minute to dissolve the cubes. Add the mandarin juice from the can then make up to 500 ml (18 fl oz) with cold water. Chill in the fridge until almost set – about 1 hour.

2 Whisk the evaporated milk in a large bowl until very foamy then stir in the almost-set jelly until well mixed. Chill until completely set, about 3 hours, then serve decorated with the mandarins.

Instant berry slush

ProPoints values per recipe 3
Takes 5 mins
Ⓥ ❄   **Serves 2**

1 small banana
150 g (5½ oz) low fat strawberry yogurt
200 g (7 oz) frozen sliced strawberries **and**
    blueberries

If you like ice cream, you'll love this speedy dessert that's made in seconds in the food processor or blender.

1 Slice the banana into a jug or food processor then add the yogurt and frozen berries.

2 Blend the mixture until smooth with a hand held blender or whizz it for a few seconds in a food processor or blender, then serve immediately.

Saucy lemon surprise

ProPoints values per recipe 30
15 mins prep, 40 mins baking
V   **Serves 6**

50 g (1¾ oz) low fat spread, plus extra
   for greasing
3 eggs, separated
100 g (3½ oz) caster sugar
grated zest of 1 lemon and
   juice of 2 lemons
50 g (1¾ oz) plain flour
250 ml (9 fl oz) skimmed milk
200 g pack blueberries
icing sugar, for dusting

When baked, this pudding separates to produce a soft, light and lemony sponge on top of a tangy lemon custard.

1 Preheat the oven to Gas Mark 4/180°C/fan oven 160°C and lightly grease a 20 cm (8 inch) round soufflé dish with the low fat spread. Put the egg whites in a bowl and whisk with an electric mixer until stiff. In a separate bowl, beat the sugar with the lemon zest and juice, egg yolks and flour. Gradually beat in the milk to make a batter.

2 Lightly fold the egg whites into the batter then pour into the soufflé dish. Put in a roasting tin half filled with hot water and bake in the oven for 40 minutes until set and golden on top, but with a lemon custard beneath. Top with the blueberries, dust with the icing sugar and serve.

Pineapple upside down cake

ProPoints values per recipe 27
10 mins prep, 30 mins baking

 Makes 8 slices

50 g (1¾ oz) low fat spread, plus a little
 for greasing
4 canned pineapple rings in natural juice
 plus 2 tablespoons of the juice
5 glacé cherries, halved
50 g (1¾ oz) light muscovado sugar
100 g (3½ oz) self raising flour
½ teaspoon vanilla extract
2 eggs
1 teaspoon baking powder
1 teaspoon clear honey

You'll love this updated retro recipe, originally from the 1970s.

1 Preheat the oven to Gas Mark 4/180°C/fan oven 160°C. Line the base of a 17 cm (6½ inch) round cake tin with some baking parchment and lightly grease the sides with a little of the low fat spread. Arrange the pineapple rings on the base of the tin, cutting them to fit if necessary, and fill in the spaces left with the halved glacé cherries.

2 Put the low fat spread, sugar, flour and vanilla extract in a bowl with the eggs and baking powder and beat with a hand held electric whisk until smooth. Whisk in 2 tablespoons of the pineapple juice to make a batter then pour over the pineapple and bake for 30 minutes, until firm when tested with a skewer.

3 Carefully turn out, drizzle with the honey and serve warm as a pudding or cold as a cake.

Blueberry poached pears

ProPoints values per recipe 10
Takes 35 mins + 1 hr chilling

 Serves 4

1 lemon
85 g (3 oz) caster sugar
3 bay leaves
4 large pears, peeled, cored and halved
150 g (5½ oz) blueberries

Pears taste completely different when poached, as they readily absorb flavours. If you want to serve these for a dinner party, keep them whole for a more dramatic effect. Serve on their own or with a 60 g (2 oz) scoop of low fat vanilla ice cream per person, for an additional 2 **ProPoints** values per serving.

1 Using a vegetable peeler, peel the zest from the lemon, put it in a large pan with 300 ml (10 fl oz) water and all the lemon juice. Add the sugar and bay leaves and simmer over a gentle heat for 10 minutes.

2 Scoop the lemon zest from the pan with a slotted spoon then add the pear halves to the liquid. Cover the pan and poach for 10 minutes until they are just tender.

3 Tip in the blueberries and cook for 2 minutes more until they are tender, but still retain their shape. Chill in the fridge for 1 hour before serving.

> *Try this* Instead of the lemon, use 1 tablespoon of balsamic vinegar for no additional **ProPoints** values per serving. The dark, syrupy, cask-aged vinegar from Moderna in Italy is surprisingly good in sweet dishes like this.

Pear and chocolate mousse cake

4 egg whites
75 g (2¾ oz) caster sugar
¼ teaspoon vanilla extract
25 g (1 oz) plain flour
3 tablespoons cocoa powder
410 g can pear halves in natural juice,
  drained
½ teaspoon icing sugar, for dusting

Pears and chocolate make a great combination and this is easy to rustle up from a few storecupboard ingredients.

1 Preheat the oven to Gas Mark 4/180°C/fan oven 160°C. Line the base and sides of a 20 cm (8 inch) round cake tin with non stick baking parchment.

2 Whisk the egg whites with an electric whisk in a clean, grease-free bowl, gradually beating in the sugar until it is thick and glossy.

3 Add the vanilla and whisk briefly to mix it in. Sift over the flour and cocoa powder and gently stir in with a metal spoon.

4 Pour into the tin then arrange the pear halves on top. Bake for 20 minutes until firm around the edge, but still a little soft in the centre when tested with a skewer. Cool in the tin then carefully turn out, and dust with the little icing sugar. Serve with the remaining pear juice spooned over.

> *Try this* For a black cherry version, replace the **pears** with fresh stoned **cherries**, for the same **ProPoints** values per serving.

Summer fruit meringue

500 g bag mixed frozen fruits
  (i.e. a mixture of blackberries, morello
  cherries, strawberries, raspberries and
  currants), thawed
50 g (1¾ oz) white or brown bread, diced
40 g (1½ oz) caster sugar

For the meringue
2 egg whites
50 g (1¾ oz) caster sugar

This tastes impressive, yet it's surprisingly simple to make. The topping is soft like a lemon meringue pie, while the base is tangy like a summer pudding.

1 Preheat the oven to Gas Mark 6/200°C/fan oven 180°C. Tip the fruits and their juices into the base of an ovenproof dish and stir in the bread and sugar.

2 To make the meringue, whisk the egg whites with an electric whisk in a clean, grease-free bowl until stiff. Gradually beat in the sugar, a tablespoon at a time, until thick and glossy.

3 Spoon evenly over the fruit, taking care not to knock out the air then bake for about 6–8 minutes to lightly brown the top. The meringue will be hot, but the fruits should be just warm below. Serve immediately.

> *Cook's tip* Although you can use either white or brown bread, white bread makes this dessert look very pretty.

Rhubarb 'n' custard pudding

ProPoints values per recipe 28
10 mins prep, 40 mins baking
V **Serves 6**

50 g (1¾ oz) low fat spread, plus a little
    for greasing
500 g (1 lb 2 oz) rhubarb, cut into lengths
grated zest and juice of 1 orange
100 g (3½ oz) caster sugar
50 g (1¾ oz) self raising flour
15 g (½ oz) custard powder
½ teaspoon baking powder
2 eggs

A little custard powder is added to the cake batter to create a classic flavour combination. It's delicious served with a 60 g (2 oz) scoop of low fat ice cream per person, for an additional 2 **ProPoints** values per serving.

1 Preheat the oven to Gas Mark 6/200°C/fan oven 180°C. Lightly grease a 17 x 23 cm (6½ x 9 inch) ovenproof dish with the low fat spread, then pile the rhubarb into the base. Mix in the zest and juice of the orange along with half of the sugar.

2 Bake for 10 minutes, stir well, then bake for another 10 minutes until the rhubarb is tender. Remove from the oven and turn down to Gas Mark 4/180°C/fan oven 160°C.

3 Tip the remaining sugar into a bowl and add the low fat spread, flour, custard powder, baking powder and eggs. Beat well, then pour the batter over the rhubarb and bake for 20 minutes until risen and pale golden.

> *Try this* When rhubarb isn't in season, you can use this topping with lightly stewed Bramley **apples** instead, for the same **ProPoints** values per person.

ProPoints value index